The Universe

Sun and Stars

Anne Welsbacher
ABDO & Daughters

Published by Abdo & Daughters, 4940 Viking Drive, Suite 622, Edina, Minnesota 55435.

Printed in the United States.

Cover and Interior Photo credits: Peter Arnold, Inc.
                         Archive Photos
Edited by Bob Italia

Library of Congress Cataloging-in-Publication Data

Welsbacher, Anne, 1955-
Sun and Stars / Anne Welsbacher
p. cm. — (The universe)
Includes index.
Summary: Discusses the location, characteristics, and uses of the sun, the closest star, and identifies other kinds of stars and how they are different.
ISBN 1-56239-722-2
1. Sun—Juvenile literature. 2. Stars—Juvenile literature. [1. Sun. 2. Stars.] I. Title. II. Series: Welsbacher, Anne. 1955- Universe.
QB521.5.W45 1997
523.8--dc20   96-26776
                                                              CIP
                                                              AC

ABOUT THE AUTHOR
Anne Welsbacher is the director of publications for the Science Museum of Minnesota. She has written and edited science books and articles for children, and has written for national and regional publications on science, the environment, the arts, and other topics.

Contents

The Sun 4

Levels of the Sun 6

Sun Storms 8

The Sun's Light 10

The Closest Star 12

Giants and Supergiants 14

More Stars 16

Beginnings and Endings 18

Sun and Star Facts 20

Glossary 22

Index 24

The Sun

The Sun is 865,400 miles (1,392,000 km) across—wide enough to fit 400 Moons.

The Sun is 93 million miles (150 million km) from the Earth. At its surface, the Sun is 10,000 degrees F (5,500 C). At the center, it is hundreds of times hotter! Most of the Sun is made up of **hydrogen** gas.

The Sun spins like a top. Some parts actually spin faster than other parts! This is possible because the Sun is made of gases.

Opposite page: A solar eruption taken from Skylab 2.

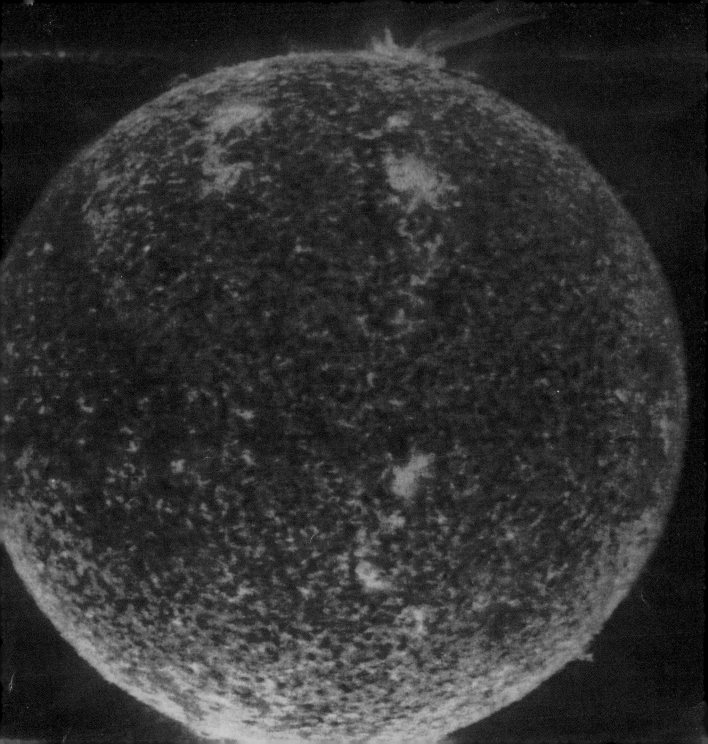

Levels of the Sun

The Sun's center, or core, is 27 million degrees (15 million C), and very heavy. The Sun's energy comes from its core.

The Sun's surface is called the **photosphere**. The light we see and the heat we feel on Earth come from this level of the Sun. **Sunspots** also form here.

Above the photosphere is the **chromosphere**. Much of the Sun's "weather" takes place at this level, including **solar flares**.

The **corona** is the Sun's top layer. Here, gases drift into space and become **solar wind**.

Opposite page: The Sun's temperature levels.

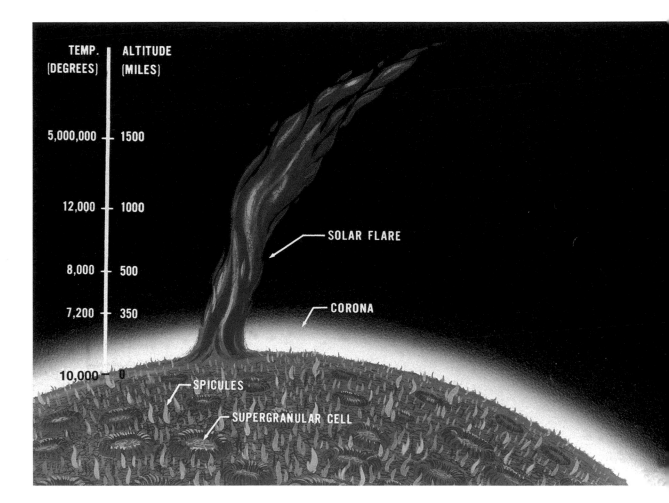

TEMP. (DEGREES) | ALTITUDE (MILES)

5,000,000 — 1500

12,000 — 1000

8,000 — 500

7,200 — 350

10,000 — 0

SOLAR FLARE

CORONA

SPICULES

SUPERGRANULAR CELL

Sun Storms

The Sun's hot gases move around very fast. This fast action causes solar storms: **sunspots**, **flares**, and **prominences**.

Sunspots are smaller areas of cooler gas that do not shine as brightly as the rest of the Sun. This makes them look like dark spots on the Sun's surface.

Flares are very hot rays of gas that **erupt** from the surface. They look like giant flames blowing off the Sun.

Prominences are thicker, longer, and bigger than flares. They look like giant loops rolling along the Sun's edge.

Opposite page: The Sun during a solar eruption.

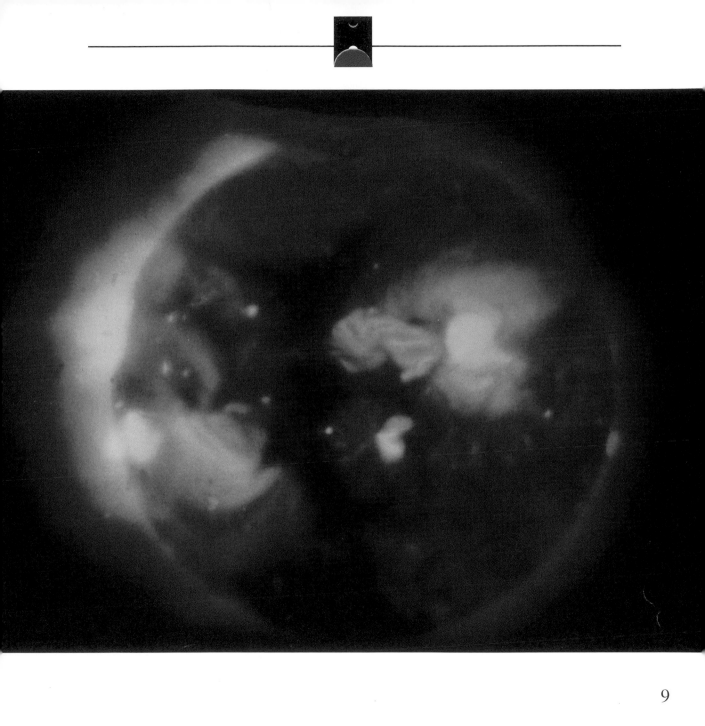

9

The Sun's Light

The Sun's heat creates **nuclear reactions** which make the light we see and the heat we feel.

On Earth, sunlight helps plants grow. The plants become food for animals. Plants also use sunlight to make **oxygen**, which animals breathe.

The Sun's heat changes our weather. Heat turns some of the water on Earth into clouds. This is called **evaporation**. Then the water in clouds falls to the Earth as rain. The Sun also heats up the air and creates wind.

The Sun makes energy we turn into **electricity**. People also use the Sun to tell time. Sundials and other objects mark the hours using the Sun's shadow.

A sundial marks the hours using the Sun's shadow.

11

The Closest Star

The Sun is one of 200 billion billion stars in the **universe**. (If all these stars were grains of sand, they would fill the ocean beaches from Maine to Florida.) The Sun is also part of a large group of stars that form the Milky Way. The Milky Way is one of billions of **galaxies**.

There are many different kinds of stars. They are grouped by color, size, heat, brightness, age, and weight. They might be blue, red, white, yellow, or other colors.

The Sun is an **ordinary star**. Some stars are smaller, but many are larger.

Opposite page: All-sky view of the Milky Way galaxy viewed from Australia.

Giants and Supergiants

Red giants are big, red stars. **Supergiants** are even larger. One hundred Suns could fit into a supergiant.

Many supergiants are blue or white because they are very hot. Sirius, in the **constellation** Canis Major, is a supergiant.

Red giants and supergiants burn their **hydrogen** in a short time. As this happens, they **expand**. If our Sun were a red giant, its edge would reach past Earth—and all the way to Mars!

Opposite page: The red giant Antares (right-center).

More Stars

Most of the stars in the sky—including the Sun—are **ordinary stars**. They are smaller than **red giants** and **supergiants**. They can be blue, red, white, yellow, or other colors.

Red dwarf stars are smaller than ordinary stars. These red stars burn very slowly and for a long time before using up their **hydrogen**.

Variable stars change in brightness. When they are young they do not shine brightly. As they age, they become brighter.

Most stars are **binary** stars. That means two stars **orbit** each other. The Sun is unusual because it is not a binary star.

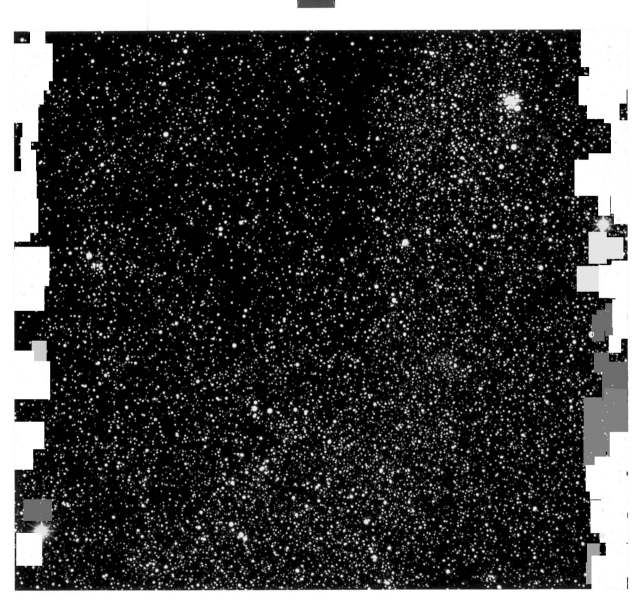

**Alpha and Beta Centauri (upper right)
are the closest stars to the Sun.**

Beginnings and Endings

Stars form from large clouds of gas and dust pulled together by **gravity**. These clouds eventually form balls which heat up. Then they shine as stars.

As stars age, they burn up all their gases while their outsides cool down. When this happens, they **expand** like a balloon and become **red giants**. The cool, outer layer eventually floats away. The remaining core then becomes a **white dwarf**, which is about the size of the Earth.

Some expanding stars become **supergiants** which can explode into **supernovae**. The most famous supernova exploded in 1054 and created the **Crab Nebula**, which can be seen in the sky.

After a supernova explosion, a star's remains might **compress** into a **neutron star**. A neutron star is only 12 miles (20 km) across. Yet it is as heavy as the Sun.

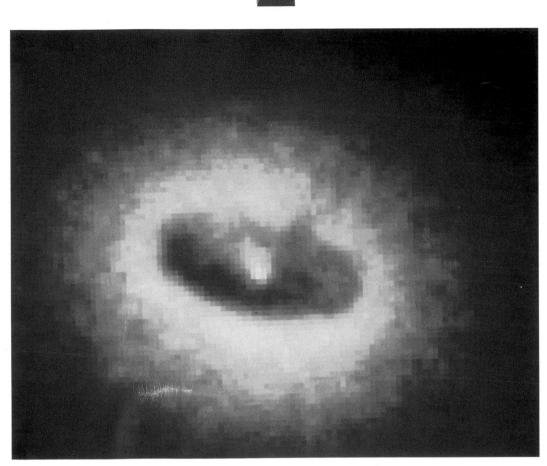

The Hubble Space Telescope shows a possible black hole.

If a star's remains **compress** even more, its **gravity** might be too strong for light to escape. Then the star becomes an invisible **black hole**.

Sun and Star Facts

Brightest star (not including the Sun) .. Sirius

Stars in the universe................................. 200 billion billion

Nearest star (not including the Sun) .... Proxima Centauri

Largest stars .... 1 billion miles across
                                    (1.6 billion km) across

Smallest stars .... 10 miles (16 km) across

Sun's distance from Earth........................ 93 million miles
                                    (1.5 million km)

Sun's age .... 4.6 billion years

Sun's expected life .... 5 billion more years

Opposite page: A supernova in the Large Magellanic Cloud.

Glossary

balance—forces of equal strength.

binary (BYE-nuh-ree) **stars**—two stars that orbit each other.

black hole—a heavenly object that may form after a supernova explosion.

chromosphere (CROW-muss-fear)—a layer of gases above the surface of the Sun.

compress—to squeeze together.

constellation (kahn-stuh-LAY-shun)—a group of stars that forms a recognized pattern.

corona—a layer of gases above the Sun's chromosphere.

Crab Nebula—the remains of a supernova explosion found in the constellation Taurus.

electricity (e-leck-TRIS-uh-tee)—a form of energy that can make light, heat, or motion.

erupt—to burst forth.

evaporation (e-vap-uh-RAY-shun)—when something turns into a gas.

expand—to stretch out.

galaxy (GAL-uck-see)—a group of billions of stars forming one system.

gravity (GRAV-uh-tee)—the natural force that causes objects to move toward the center of heavenly bodies.

hydrogen (HI-druh-jen)—a gas; hydrogen makes up most of a star.

neutron (NEW-tron) **star**—a type of star; very small and heavy.

nuclear reaction (NEW-klee-ir ree-AK-shun)—the process that creates energy from matter.

orbit—the path of any heavenly body aound another heavenly body.

ordinary stars—the most common stars in the universe. They are smaller than red giants and supergiants, and can be blue, red, white, yellow, or other colors.

oxygen (OX-ih-jen)—a gas without color, taste, or smell that helps make air and water.

photosphere (FOE-toes-fear)—the surface of the Sun.

prominences (PROM-ih-nen-sez)—rays of gas that shoot off the Sun.

red giant—a type of star; among the largest kinds.

solar flare—very hot rays of gas that shoot off the Sun.

solar wind—created by the Sun when gases in its corona drift into space.

sunspots—dark areas in the Sun's atmosphere that are not as hot or bright as other areas.

supergiant—a type of star; the largest type.

supernova—the explosion of a dying star.

universe (YEW-nih-vers)—everything found in space.

variable (VAIR-e-uh-bull) **stars**—stars that change in brightness.

white dwarf—a type of star; smaller and cooler than most.

Index

A

age 12, 18
animals 10

B

binary stars 16
black hole 19
brightness 12

C

Canis Major 14
chromosphere 6
clouds 10, 18
colors 12, 14, 16
constellation 14
core 6, 18
corona 6
Crab Nebula 18

D

dust 18

E

Earth 4, 10, 14, 18, 20
electricity 10
energy 6
evaporation 10

F

flares 8

G

galaxies 12
gases 4, 6, 8, 18
giants 14, 16
gravity 18, 19

H

heat 6, 10, 12, 18
hydrogen 14, 16

K

kinds 12

L

light 6, 10

M

Mars 14
Milky Way 12
moon 4

N

neutron stars 18
nuclear reactions 10

O

ordinary stars 12, 16
oxygen 10

P

photosphere 6
plants 10
prominences 8

R

rain 10
red dwarfs 16
red giants 14, 18

S

Sirius 14
size 12
solar flares 6
solar storms 8
solar wind 6
sundials 10
sunspots 6, 8
supergiants 14, 16, 18
supernovae 18
surface 4, 8

T

temperature 4, 6, 14

U

universe 12

V

variable stars 16

W

water 10
weather 10
weight 6, 12
white dwarfs 18
wind 10